# A Brief Introduction to Arunachal Pradesh

Kaushik Bhagawati
R. Bhagawati
Doni Jini
R.A. Alone
R. Singh
A. Chandra
(kaushik.iasri@gmail.com)

**2016**

Published by

Authors
With due permission from:
ICAR Research Complex for NEH Region
Arunachal Pradesh Centre, Basar-791101
(kaushik.iasri@gmail.com)

# Preface

Arunachal Pradesh, formerly known as North East Frontier Agency (NEFA), is the land of rising sun of India. It is endowed with rich biological and cultural diversity. It is entirely a hilly state lies on the mighty Himalayan and Patkoi ranges. It is inhabitant of 26 major tribes and 110 sub-tribes with wide ranges of culture, rituals, religion and habits. The state comes under Indo-Myanmar biodiversity zone with centre of origin of several crops and is termed as "Paradise of Botanist."

This book is intended for those who want to get preliminary information about this beautiful Himalayan state. This is not about political or current knowledge of Arunachal Pradesh, but about Arunachal Pradesh as it was and as it is. We try to give a brief note on geography, history, people, culture, rituals and practices. This is also for those who want to spend little money for the sake of knowledge.

**Authors**

# Acknowledgement

First of all we all bow our head in front of All Mighty God and our parents for giving us all the blessings and strength for the endeavour.

We are grateful to our hon'ble Director Dr. S.V. Ngachan for being the constant source of encouragement for us in all our works and activities. He is a real scientist and visionary.

We are thankful to all the staff of ICAR A.P. Centre, Basar for their support and help during the work. Special thanks to Mr. Amit Sen, Mr. Kshitiz Kumar Shukla and Mr. Bharat Singh.

Thank you all

Authors

# Contents

# 1

# Brief Geography

*(Land, Climate, Soil and Nature)*

**Land**

Arunachal Pradesh is situated in the North Eastern region of India between 26.28°N and 29.30°N latitude and 91.20°E and 97.30°E longitude. Area-wise, it is largest state of the region with total geographical area of 83,743 square kilometres. It has common international boundary with Bhutan, China and Myanmar. The entire state lies on the mighty Himalayan and Patkoi ranges. The elevation of the hills ranges from 60 meters to over 7000 meters. Mt. Kangto (7090 m), Mt. Nyegi Kangsang (7050 m) and Mt. Gorichen (6488 m) are three highest peaks of Arunachal Pradesh. The Himalayan mountain system divides the state mainly into five river valleys: the Kameng, the Subansiri, the Siang, the Lohit and the Tirap. These rivers, along with innumerable rivulets traversing through innumerable hill systems treading through the rugged terrains, steep hills, valleys and ultimately drain down to from two major river systems and valleys of the region- the Brahmaputra and the Barak. Among these rivers, the mightiest is the Siang (also called the Dihang) river that originates from China as Tsangpo in Tibet and become the Brahmaputra in Assam, combining with the other rivers. The rivers possess vast hydroelectricity generation potential of 20, 000 Mega Watt, and but are unfit for navigation.

The area of Arunachal Pradesh can be broadly grouped into four distinct physiographic regions:

1. The greater Himalayas with snow capped mountains with altitude ranging up to above 7,000 meters,

2. Lower Himalayas ranges up to 3,500 meters of altitude,

3. The sub-Himalayan belt including Siwalik hills, the altitude ranging up to 1,700 meters, and

4. The plains which are eastern continuity of Assam plains.

Out of the total area of the state, broad and narrow valleys constitute 35 per cent each, the foot hills and the plains cover 10 percent and the snow clad peaks, approximately covers 20 per cent.

Geologically, the major rock formation in Arunachal Pradesh can be grouped into Tertiary, Gondwana, Unfossiliferous sediments and Metamorphites.

**Climate**

Because of varied topography and unique position in the Indian subcontinent, the state of Arunachal Pradesh has lot of climatic variation. In terms of rainfall, the climate of Arunachal Pradesh can be said to be Per-Humid. It is one of the highest rainfall recipient states of the country with more than 3500 mm in a year. The state receives rainfall over a period of 8 to 9 months excepting in winter, however, most of rainfall is between May and September. Higher regions experience snow fall during winter. The average annual rainfall is 1000 mm in the higher elevations and 5750 mm in the foot hill areas. This diversity in the climate and also in topography accounts for wide diversity in vegetation and agriculture. The normal temperature during winter months varies between 15ºC to 21ºC, while it varies from 22ºC to 33ºC during monsoon months. In the summer months the temperature sometime reaches to around 40ºC in foot hills of the state.

Arunachal Pradesh comes under Eastern Himalayan Ecozone-II. Agro-climatically it is divided into five zones:

1.  Alpine Zone (18.5%),
2.  Temperate Sub-Alpine Zone (27.6%),
3.  Sub-Tropical Hill Zone (25.7%),
4.  Mid-Tropical Hill Zone (7.6%), and

5. Mid-Tropical Plain Zone (20.6%)

As per the temperature and rainfall, the agroclimatic sub-regions of Arunachal Pradesh are as follows:

1. Humid Hyperthermic Foothills:

2. Perhumid Hyperthermic Foothills

3. Thermic Perhumid Midhills and Valleys

4. Thermic Humid Midhills and Valleys

5. Alpine and High Hills

Thus, it provides potential environment and condition for growth of wide variety of crops ranging from temperate to tropical.

**Land Use**

Around 5.15 million hectares (61.54%) is under forests. The arable land (the net area sown plus the current & fallow lands) is estimated at 0.25 million hectares (3.08%) of the total reporting area (8.37 million ha). Land under miscellaneous tree crops and groves, not included in the net area sown, is 0.04 million hectares (0.53%) and the culturable waste-land is 0.03 million hectares (0.4%) of the total reporting area.

**Soil**

The wide diversity in climate, physiography, geology and vegetation influenced the formation of different kind of soils in Arunachal Pradesh. The National Bureau of Soil Survey & Land Use Planning, Regional Centre, Jorhat, the major categories of the soils is as under:

1. <u>Soils of Warm per-Humid (Eastern Himalayan Ecosystem):</u> The ecozone constitutes, the major areas in the state, covering Tawang, most part of East and West Kameng district, Lower and Upper

Subansiri belts except southern part, East and West Siang, Dibang Valley and northern part of Lothit, occupying around 80 per cent of the geographical area. Natural vegetation comprises alpine and sub-alpine, temperate (Coniferous), semi evergreen and tropical moist deciduous forests. The soils of summits and ridges are mostly shallow, moderately shallow to deep, loamy skeletal to sandy skeletal, excessively drained and subject to severe to very severe erosion hazards. Most of the soils show lack of profile development. The texture varies from gravelly loam to gravelly sandy loam, taxonomically classified as Lithic and Typic Udorthents, Entic Haplumbrepts, Dystrict

Eutrochrepts, Unbric and typic Dystrochrepts.

The soils are strongly to moderately acidic in nature, rich in organic matter and generally have low base saturation except some soils in summits and ridges. The soils are rich in organic matter. The region is typified by *Udic* soil moisture regime with availability of soil moisture exceeding 270 days and in *Thermic* soil temperature regimes (18°C to 22°C mean annual soil temperature).

2. <u>Soils of Warm per-Humid, Siwalik Hill Ecosystem</u>: The ecozone covers the areas constituting the southern part of West and East Kameng district, Lower and Upper Subansiri and part of West Siang District. It

constitutes around 7.4 percent of the total geographical area of the state. The natural vegetation comprises wet evergreen and tropical moist deciduous forests. The area represents *Udic* soil moisture regime and *Hyper thermic* soil temperature regime. The soils are moderately acidic in nature having medium to high organic matter content, high exchangeable aluminium content and very poor in base saturation.

3. <u>Soils of Warm per-Humid, North-Eastern Hill Ecosystems</u>: The eco-zone comprises the north-eastern part of the state constituting Tirap, Changlang, and some part of Lohit belt. It occupies 0.44 million hectares, comprising 5.3% of the total geographical area of the state. The area

represents Udic soil moisture regime and *Hyper thermic* in the valleys and low hill ranges and *Thermic* in high hill ranges. The natural vegetation comprises wet evergreen and tropical moist deciduous forests. The soils are strongly to moderately acidic in nature, high in organic matter content, high in exchangeable aluminium and very poor in base saturation.

4. <u>Soil of Hot Humid Ecozone (Assam Plain Ecosystem)</u>: The eco-zone comprising, the plains of the Brahmaputra river systems which is the eastern continuity of Assam plains and covers parts of Lohit, Dibang Valley, Tirap and East Siang District of the state. It occupies around 0.6 million hectares, constituting 7.1 per cent of the

total geographical area of the state. The climate of the area is characterised by hot summers and moderately cool winters. The soil moisture regime by *Udic* and the area qualifies *Hyper thermic* soil temperature regime with a mean annual soil temperature of 22°C and higher. The natural vegetation comprises semi evergreen and moist deciduous forests. The soils on upper pedimont, upland and gently sloping plains are moderately to slightly acidic in nature having moderate to high organic matter content, moderate to poor in base saturation. On the contrary, the soils on flood plain areas are slightly acidic to mildly alkaline in nature with high base saturation.

## Nature

Arunachal Pradesh is the region where the pre-Tertiary Tethys Sea first began to close, opening up a pathway for the Palaeoarctic biota of Tibet and Malayan elements from the South east, which resulted in enormous ecological and floristic diversity. Owing to its rich biological diversity, the state is regarded as the *'Paradise of the Botanists.'* Humid tropical, sub-tropical, temperate and alpine zones influenced by high rainfall, varying temperature, humidity and wide ranging soil and physico-geographical situation have made this region as one of the "Mega-Biodiversity Hot-Spots" in the world and is the centre of origin of number of cultivated plants. The state comes under the Indo-Myanmar biodiversity zone. The state is custodian of 23.52 per cent of total flowering plants of India including around 4,500 species of angiosperm and 550 species of orchids; and is also regarded as nature's repository of medicinal plants where around 500 medicinal plants were identified during preliminary survey. Arunachal Pradesh possesses India's second highest level of genetic resources. The region has been identified by Indian Council of Agricultural Research (ICAR) as the centre of rice germplasm, while National Bureau of Plant Genetic Resources (NBPGR) has highlighted the region being rich in wild relatives of crop plants. It is the centre of origin of citrus crops. The fauna diversity includes 85 species of mammals and 760 species of birds.

# 2
# People
# &
# Culture
*(Tribes, Language, Religion and Festivals)*

## Tribes and language

Arunachal Pradesh is the home of 26 major tribes and 110 sub-tribes, with about two third of population comes under schedule tribes that are indigenous to the state. The majority of the native tribes trace their origin from the Tibeto-Burman origin. There is a large cultural and ethonolinguistic division within the state. In the most western part, the dominated group are the *Monpa* tribe with several sub-tribes speaking closely related but mutually incomprehensible languages. Majority of the *Monpas* and sub-tribes practices Buddhism. The north-central part also known as the *Tani* area, the major tribes is Nishi that include *Bangni*, *Tagin* and even *Hills Miri*. Though *Apatani* tribe is also included under Nishi tribes, but they are culturally and linguistically very different. *Apatani* tribe is considered to be the most advanced tribes in the state. Towards east-central part, the major tribe is *Galo* with lot of sub-tribes, mainly *Lare* and *Pugo*. The *Adi* tribes are the largest tribe of Arunachal Pradesh with major division as *Padam, Pasi, Minyong* and *Bokar*. Tribe like Milang are included under the *Adi* tribe, but they are culturally very distinct. The

*Mishmi* cultural-linguistic area of the east comprise of tribes like *Idu, Miju* and *Digaru* with wide mutual variations in culture and lifestyle. One of the unique tribal groups is the *Tai Khamti* with wide variation from the rest of the tribes of Arunachal Pradesh. They are religiously similar to the *Chakmas* who have migrated from Bangladesh, practicing the *Theraveda* sect of Buddhism. The *Singpho* and Tangsa tribes exhibit much similarity with the culture of Myanmar. The *Nocte* and *Wangcho* tribes have close resemblance with the *Nagas* of the Nagaland.

Each tribes and sub-tribes have their own language that is in turn distinct from the other even within the same group. Some languages within the group are mutually incomprehensible. The major languages are *Nishi, Dafla, Miji, Adi,*

*Gallong, Wancho, Tagin, Hill Miri, Mishumi, Mompa, Nockte, Aka, Tangsa, Khampti, Serdukpen* etc.

## Religion

The major religion of the state includes Christianity, Hindu, Buddhism, and indigenous religion mainly *Dyoni Polo*. The percentage of Christianity is highest in the state. Buddhism is found among the *Mompas* and related tribes in Tawang, West Kameng and Upper Siang District. It is also prevalent among the Khamti tribes in the eastern part.

*Dyoni Polo* is unique religion confined in Arunachal Pradesh. It is the indigenous religions, of animistic and shamanic type, of the *Tani* and other Tibeto-Burman people. *Donyi-Polo* is related to the *Hemphu-Mukrang* religion of the *Karbi* and the *Nyezi-No* of the *Hruso*. There is no written scripture for *Donyi-Poloism*. But there are numerous hymns and myths on the faith handed down from generation to generation (*Abans*). According to the belief system, *Doni Bote* or simply *Tani* or human being is conceived to be the ultimate material outcome of the grand spiritual evolution. *Sedi Dimyang myane* is the originator of all the objects in the cosmos and being on the earth. He handed down emissaries to govern various domains of his spiritual empire. Gods and Goddesses that rule the periphery of the earth and hundreds and thousands of lives on our planet are believed to have emerged through the womb of *Pedong Nane*. Main deities under Dony-Poloism are:

- *Konki Boke*: God who designed the physical forms of man.

- *Kine Mone (Kine Nane)* is the spiritual mother of fertility, productivity and contentment of the tribe. She reins the world beneath the earth. It is on here pleasure, human being reap crops and free themselves from poverty and hunger.

- *Daadi Bote* is the God of tamed animals, especially *mithuns*. It is he who sent down the first mithun to human society, remembered during *Solung* festival. A whole night is devoted to narrated story about him and acquisition of *mithuns* by *Miris* in *Limir-Libon Aabang*. *Polung Sobo* is also a spiritualised image of a great *mithun.* Two more image from *Diling* i.e. *Limir Sobo* and *Karpung Karduk.*

- *Robo (Taro)* rules over deep jungle (forest). Trees, creepers, gorses, birds and animals of the Jungle, are the properties of *Robo*. *Epom* or *Yapom* (spirit of the deep forest), is believed to be the descendant of *Robo*.

- *Biri Bote* is the main spirit of water, who causes soil erosion on river bank. The *Adis* believe that *Biri Bote* in the form of *Biri Biak* moves with high flood current and commands waves and current to knock against the bank and cause erosion. He is very much feared by tribe. *Ladang Bote* is the spirit of deep water.

- *Dimu Bote* lives in snow clad peaks and rules over entire snow falling areas of the earth. All the herbs, animals including birds living there is his properties. *Nomgu Bote* controls the domain of sickness, poverty suffering through Jungle animals, insects, birds, pests and their agents. If he is displeased, he may send or release wild animals, birds and insects to cause menace to standing crops.

A person who lived a life of truthfulness, amity, understanding, selflessness, and purity obtains straight flight to the land of *Donyi Polo* or light and peace.

**Festivals**

Here by festival we mean an event ordinarily celebrated by a community and cantering on some characteristic aspect of the community and its religion or traditions

(Wikipedia). The people of Arunachal Pradesh are festival loving and beside religion, the significant origin of their festivals is agriculture. They celebrate various annual and seasonal festivals closely knitted in their agrarian society. Out of 110 festivals celebrated by different tribes, around 60 are associated with agriculture. To please their deity, they sacrifice animals (*mithuns*, cow, pig, poultry etc) and nourish themselves with meat organizing community feast.

The festivals are generally divided into three categories: (i) Purely Religious, (ii) Religio-Agricultural and (iii) Purely Agricultural. The festivals are distributed throughout the year depending on the agricultural and seasonal cycles.

The festival calendar of different tribes of Arunachal Pradesh is given as below which is broadly divided into those purely religious in nature and those that are related to agriculture:

### 1. Purely Religious

| January | |
|---|---|
| **Tribe** | **Festival** |
| Kahampti | Niching Tim-Mum |
| Apatani | Morung |
| Nishi | Lingdi Puja |
| Monpa | Torgya |
| **February** | |
| Singpho | Magata |
| Idu Mishmis | Reh |
| Adi | Hurin Monam |
| **March** | |
| Nishi | Nyokum Yellow |
| Singpho | Khati |
| Apatani | Myoko |
| Monpa | Losar Khachol |
| Monpa | Chepche |
| **April** | |
| Wancho | Sasaban |
| Singhpho | Rata |
| **May** | |
| Singpho | Watta |
| Khampti | Nirhirk Tim-Mum |
| Adi | Yelo Mola and Pale anm |
| Monpa | Ngahn and Sakadawa, Sang Dri, Soskar |
| **June** | |
| Khampti | Nuncil Tim-Mum |
| Monpa | Guru Rimpochi |
| **July** | |
| Nocte | Rogham |

24

| Singpho | Sithumte |
|---------|----------|
| Khampti | Ninpet Tim Mum |
| Sherdukpen | Wang |
| Monpa | Drukpa Tseshi |

### August

| Membas and Khembas | Gepa Chenga |
|--------------------|-------------|

### September

| Adi | Ampi Mohan |
|-----|------------|
| Adi | Pire and Yaga |
| Singpho | Simita or Chari Sitang |
| Khampti | Ninchi Tim-Mum |

### October

| Singpho | Gupsite |
|---------|---------|
| Khampti | Nicip-et-Tim-Mum |
| Adi | Pine and Yaga |
| Monpa | Lhabab Dhinichen |

### November

| Singpho | Guptumgra |
|---------|-----------|
| Khampti | Nichin-Tim-Mun |
| Adi | Habo Panam |
| Adi | Doring |
| Monpa | Gupa Chababduichan |
| Sherdukpen | Wang |

### December

| Membas and Khembas | Denba Chuk |
|--------------------|------------|
| Khawa | Khyat Sowai |
| Monpa | Garden Ngacho and Nyanpagazon |
| Sherdukpen | Khiksaba |

## 2. Agriculture and Agri-religious

### January

| Tribes | Festivals |
|--------|-----------|
| Wancho | Wan-Gak |

25

| | |
|---|---|
| Nocte | Khetipuja |
| Nishi | Si-Donyl |

## February

| | |
|---|---|
| Wancho | Oriah |
| Tangsa | Mol |
| Khampti | Nincam-Tim-Mum |
| Adi | Mopin, Donging puja |
| Membas and Khembas | Donging puja |
| Mishmis | Ali-aya-Ligangs |
| Nishi | Nyokum Yellow |
| Hill Miri | Buri Boot |
| Miji | Khan |
| Aka | Sarok |
| Nishi (Bangris) | Myokum |

## March

| | |
|---|---|
| Wancho | Ojiyele |
| Digaru Mishmis | Tamala Ddn. |
| Miji Mishmis | Takka thong |
| Nishi | Ebboo, Mipkom Yalo |
| Hill Miri | Buri Boot |

## April

| | |
|---|---|
| Nocte | Orang |
| Wancho | Tap-Gat, Chatchaban |
| Tangsa | Lamrong Poi |
| Adi (Padam) | Lutor or Etor |
| Adi (Minyong) | Etor |
| Adi (Gallong) | Mopin |
| Nishi | Solung, Miokum |
| Sulung | Solung |

## May

| | |
|---|---|
| Wancho (Panchow) | Tathaban |
| Wancho (Longding) | Howjojing |
| Tangsa | Howoimo |
| Adi | Monpum Puja |
| Sherdukpen | Chekar or Soskar |

### June

| | |
|---|---|
| Nocte | Loku |
| Wandro (Wakka) | Howjnging |
| Adi | Solng |
| Apatani | Myokum |

### July

| | |
|---|---|
| Tangsa (Kamloo) | Cham Mo-Poi |
| Tangsa (Yamchom) | Parong Mo and Hat rong Kah |
| Adis | Solung |
| Apatani | Dree |

### August

| | |
|---|---|
| Adi (Padam) | Solung Ponung |
| Apatani | Yaoung Puja |
| Monpa | Song Diri Jigieh |

### September

| | |
|---|---|
| Wancho (Wakka) | Khakamgai |
| Adi (Minyong) | Pombi and Solung |
| Nishi | Nyokum |

### October

| | |
|---|---|
| Wnacho | Loymphom |
| Mijis | Fung Glin |

### November

| | |
|---|---|
| Nocte | Loku |
| Wancho | Colam |
| Aka | Nechido |

### December

| | |
|---|---|
| Tangsa (Murmao) | Loiphakpoi |
| Tangsa (Nampong) | Chamrung Rok |
| Nishi | Sirom Molo-Sochum |

Out of the various festivals, the *Myoko* festival of *Apatani* tribes is noteworthy. It is the

27

most lavishly drinking and eating festival celebrated two years rotation wise.

Mopin is another important festival of the state celebrated by the *Adis* and related sub-tribes. *Mopin* is celebrated once in a year during the month of March to April to mark the beginning of the cultivation weeks. *Moin Uye Pinku* and *Pinte*, mean worshiping the God and Goddesses of the wealth for prosperous cultivation, healthy growth of domestic animals and well being of human beings. Festival like *Mopin* are also celebrated by the *Nocte* in Tirap district which they call "*Loku*" or "*Chalo-Loku*", while the *Nyishi* and *Hill Miris* in Subansiri region call it by "*Nyokum*" and "*Boori Boot*" respectively. All these festivals are celebrated at the advent of spring season.

*Losar* is important festival of Buddhist community mostly celebrated in districts of Tawang and West Kameng. The festival mark the beginning of new year of *Monpa* and co-tribes, with the word '*lo*' means new and '*sar*' meaning year. The festival is celebrated in the first day of the Tibetan lunar calendar, and mostly falls on third week of February.

Another important festival of the state is *Dree* festival of *Apatanic* community, which is mainly celebrated from 5th July to 7th July and is related to agriculture. The literary meaning of '*Dree*' is one who borrows or purchases food grains from others in order to meet out the shortage by addition to one's old and new stock of food grains.

Other important festivals includes *Nyokum*, *Solung*, *Loku*, *Sanken* etc.

# 3
# Livelihood

*(Agriculture and Craft)*

## Agriculture

Agriculture is the mainstay of population of Arunachal Pradesh. Predominantly shifting cultivation is practised in a large scale in about more than 50 per cent of grossed cropped area. Some tribes like *Apatani* and *Monpa* practised settled cultivation since time immemorial. The climatic diversity and wide variation in topography provide immense potential for diversified agriculture in the state, ranging from temperate to tropical crops. The state is a rice treasurer of plant agro-biodiversity. Around 65 to 70 crop plants are grown in the state providing plenty of options and sources. The forest diversity of the state is intricately linked with crop farming and livestock domestication, which provides substantial base to meet the need of food, ethano-medicines, fodder and fuel thus sustaining the bio-cultural diversity of the communities.

The major food crops includes paddy (*Oryza sativa* L.) with wide range of local and indigenous varieties, maize (Zea mays L.), wheat (*Triticum aestivum*), barley (*Hordeum Vulgare*), kodo (*Paspalum scrobiculantum*), china millet (*Pancium miliaceum*), mandua (*Elusine coracana* Gaertn.), jowar (*Sorghum bicolor*), French bean (*Phaseolus vulgare* L.), local soybean (*Glycine soja Sieb*), lobia (*Vigna unguiculata*), mustard (*Brassica campestris* var. *nigra*), Lai patta

(*Brassica juncea* var. *cuniefolia*), job's tear (*Coix lachrymal-jobi*), red chilli (*Capsicum annuum, C. frutescens*), pea (*Pisum sativum*), Potato (*Solanum tuberosum*) etc and several tuber crops like *Colocasia esculenta, Alocasia indica*, Elephant food yam (*Amorphophallus paeoniifolius*), Cassava (Manihot esculenta), sweet potato (Ipomoea batatas) etc. Among the species crops ginger (*Zingiber officinale*), turmeric (*Curcuma longa*) and large cardamom (*Amomum subulantum* Roxb.) are grown in commercial scale in the eastern part of the state.

The state has five agro-climatic zones ranging from temperate to sub-tropical. The region is also typified by *Udic* soil moisture regime with availability of soil moisture exceeding 270 days and in *Thermic* soil temperature regimes (18 to 22°C mean annual soil temperature). This factor favours plantation of different temperate sub-tropical fruits and vegetables. Thus, the environment of Arunachal Pradesh provides suitable niches for special cultivation of fruits, vegetables, flowers, mushroom, species, medicinal and aromatic plants. The major fruits grown in the state include orange, pineapple, banana, guava, apple, walnut, strawberry, kiwi, pears, peach, passion fruit, etc. So far, there are over 500 species of medicinal plants reported in the state.

Beside crop diversity, there exists a large crop varietal diversity also occurs in the state.

**Prevalent Rice Germplasm Diversity**

Some of the important local rice germplasm cultures prevalent in various districts of Arunachal Pradesh are as enumerated in the table below:

| District | Prevalent rice germplasm culture |
|---|---|
| Tawang | Olem |
| West Kameng | Chuksing Pa, Nabeye Ne Sa, Rabalanghu, Raw, Sung, Sungha, Tongbar, Thumbara, Thumpi |
| East Kameng | Lonrow, Pakke Amm, Pany (Tari), Paru, Rallow |
| Lower Subansiri | Anka, Betjuti, End, Khilly, Amo, Nilony, Thirti, Yamuk |
| Apatani Plateau | Emo, Emo Elang, Emo Empu, Emo Enkhe, Emo Are, Emo Hat, Ji Pyat, Nipya Pyani, Mipya Pyare, Mipya Pyat, Pyaping Pyani, Mishing (*Jhum*), Owe Impo, Pyapin, Pyapin Pyankha, Pyapin Pyat, Pyaping Pyare, Pyat Kogya, Pyani, pyat Pyapu, Rode Amo |
| Upper Subansiri | Bali, Bee, Buing, Daji, Dazing (Sali), Gapu (Yapu), Goypung, Hibar Hirpu, Ke Che, Ke Ling, Lite, Pana, Pinini (Penin), Pomin, Yapu Pumik, Zingmick (Sali) |
| East Siang | Amka, Amkel Jorang, Amlong, Ampang, Amtum, Boling, Bura, Jajum, Jiko Amo, Jorang, Joya, Kasiang, Kolom Amo, Laye Amo, Letung, Longkang, Nipung, Mipung, Motum, Bora, Oiky, Pashing, Pehi, Pelu, Royila Amo, Tahsa, Tajah, Takel, Tuinu, Tumtum, Yaling, Yamuk |
| West Siang | Amte Kimin, Anker, Bali, Damgam, Jorang, Kerpu, Khamte Yali, Khilly Amo, Kimin, Lahi, Lelli, Lemuk, Lemuk Mukte, Lipu, Lite, Mede Depu, Mipun, Nami, Neuly, Ningtl, Plu Amo, Pupi (Popy), Soiki, Tabor, Tharti Ahu, Yabor, Yamuk, Yayo |
| Dibang Valley | Ahu Mali, Amdang, Amte Boro, Amyong, Asiamkel, Beera, Birabonga, Dajum, Dard, Keopu, Taying |
| Lohit | Amu, Aphu, Babang, Bor, Bora, Chomcha, Chomju, Chomkhu, Chompat, Kamplung Mang, Kamti Joha, Kauchal Mang, Kayum Mang, Ke |

| | |
|---|---|
| | Bord, Ke Huse, Ke Sa, Ke Shi, Khaunou, Khawmakhen, Khawji, Loilang, Mahjang, Maibum, Maidang, Mesong, Miyo, Nayang, Patom, Patong, Poyong, Setiseeds, Singkhan, Tahang, Tule |
| Tirap | Bakbak, Betjuti, Gamlam, Gangtah, Honai, Joha, Kanyak, Khopsan, Lahi, Longdiak, Longkhap, Maichong, Mate, Patam, Pelu, Ramlo, Sampo, Sasang, Sasian, Simoi, Tahsa, Taling, Tuinu, Wangkan, Wangkham, Wangsam, Yasing, Yummuk |

After rice, maize is second largely grown crop the state. The major land races of the maize in the state include *Tapio, Tami, Topp, Top-puli, Pui-Ritchi, Oghum, Oyusum, Fentang, Ashum and Fenlang*.

## Indigenous wild edible plants

Beside the traditional crops, the people of Arunachal Pradesh consume large number of plants from the forest or natural habitats. The predominantly consumed plant species are Amaranthus caudatus, Bauhinia purpurea,

Sphenoclea zeylanica, Ardisia grandifolia, Gentum gnemon and *Dendrocalamus hamiltoni*. The root and tuber crops collected from wild are one of the major food of the people of the state. The major root and tuber crops includes *Colocasia esculenta, Lasia sprinosa, Dioscorea glabra, D, bulbifera, D. Pentaphylla.*

The young succulent shoots of the bamboo is edible delicacy with wide social significance in the state. Traditionally the bamboo shoots are used as a food item with wide taste owing to richness of bamboo diversity in the state. The major edible bamboo plant species of the state includes *Bambusa phillida, B. tulda, Dendrocalamus giganteus, D. Hookerii, Gigantochola albociliata, Phylllostachys manii* and *Pseudostachyum polymorphum.*

**Livestock and Poultry**

The major livestock of the state includes pig, mithun (*Bos frontails*), yak (*Bos grunniens*), cattle and goat. The presence of mithun and yak, the two different species of large ruminants makes the livestock wealth of the state distinct from other parts of the country.

**Mithun**

Mithun, the semi-domesticated free-range bovine species is an important component of the livestock production system in the north-eastern state in general and Arunachal Pradesh in particular. Practically, all the tribes of Arunachal Pradesh rear mithun but their purpose and utilization differ from tribe to tribe and from place to place. It serves as a medium of fulfilment of all social, moral, religious and economic obligations of the tribes of the state. It is called "HOBO" or "SOBO" by the Galos and "ESONG" by Miyong and Nishi tribes called it as "SEBEE". In Sanskrit it is called "GAVAYA" and in hindi "GAVI." Mithun prefer cool, forested areas typically found in the altitude range of 600 to 2700 mmsl. It is well adapted to steep hill forests. This animal has religious significance and is closely related to the socio-cultural dimension. Traditionally considered as a symbol of wealth, apart from being reared for meat and highly preferred by the tribals, the animal is also a good source of superior quality milk and hide. The LURA system of temporary community confinement of the mithuns during growing seasons has wide ecological significance towards biodiversity conservation.

There is unique ownership pattern and identification of mithun. Largely mithuns belongs to individuals. In most of the cases, ownership of large herds of mithuns is held by wealthy people. While in Apatabi tribe, mithuns are owned by a family, a clan or a village. Identification of mithun is done by ear notching which is prevalent in most of the tribes of the state. Each cut is specific and quite distinct for a clan and a family and even differ from village to village. Some tribes call their animals with specific names from calfhood.

Mithun sacrifice during religious ceremonies to please the deities is prevalent throughout the state. The mithun sacrifices is done to increase productivity of crops, livestock and save human race from flood, famine and diseases. In *Idu Mishmi* tribe, the mithun is not sacrificed to the evil but a priest bargain a sacrificial animal in place of sick persons. Mithun is top most offer to sacrifice to the evil spirit in letting the sick person to recover. Mithun is also scarified by different tribes during the occasion of harvesting as during *Moram* of *Apatani*, *Nykuom* of *Nishi* etc.

During mirage, mithuns are used as the most common bride price in most of the tribes (*Adi, Apatani, Mishmi* and *Nishi*) of Arunachal Pradesh.

Mithun also play vital role in settlement of disputes or during violation of social rules and laws. In this system, both parties and clan sacrifice one mithun each. Meat is shared/distributed among the clans or villages. This is called "*Dintek*" in *Galo*, "*Dintii*" in *Nishi*. This way dispute is resolved in a local court. Mithun is also used as a mode of payment of fine for violation of social rule and bylaws, like theft, rape, murder etc.

**Yak**

Yak is very important bovines for those living in area above the altitude of 3000 msl in pastoral areas of Kameng, Tawang and Upper Subansiri districts of Arunachal Pradesh. It provides almost all the necessary inputs like milk, meat, hairs for wool, hides, and draught power etc to sustain nomadic life of the high hill inhabitants. Yak has several socio-religious significance among the tribes of Tibeto-Mangloid origin who mostly follow Buddhism. The yak herdsmen of the state adore several yak-headed deities like Yama the God of death and Yamantika-the sarver of human kind.

Pig and poultry are integral and inseparable part of the state agriculture, as most of the people depends on animal for their economic support. The scale and mode of pig and poultry production are diverse throughout Arunachal Pradesh. Around eighty percent of the pig and poultry population in the state is raised in small, privately owned backyard and free-range systems.

**Fishery**

Fish is an indispensable item of food for the tribal of Arunachal Pradesh and it is one of the most important subsidiary occupations. It is connected to religious activities involving taboos. The state has abundant water bodies suitable for fishery viz the rivers Kameng, Subansiri, Dikrong, Pachin, Rangu, Dibang, Lohit, Noadhing, Buridhing and Tirap. They are not sharply delimited, transitions are gradual and extremely dry period does not occur. All these rivers are perennial i.e flow throughout the year. There are more than 150 species of fish recorded in the state including cold water species, warm water species and mixed water species. The lotic and lentic water systems of the region have plenty of colourful fishes which are considered as ornamental or decorative fishes. The major group of ornamental fishes includes *Barbs and Minnows, Cat fishes, Eel, Gourami, Loaches, Needle Fish, Perch, Snake Head, Puffer, Knife Fish etc.*

## Crafts and Weaving

Craft and weaving are very important and indispensible part of tribal community. The tribes of Arunachal Pradesh has rich heritage of indigenous craft and weaving. The handicraft of Arunachal Pradesh is of high standard, many tribes makes their own hats which are extremely decorative, adorned with beaks and feathers of birds or with tuffs of hair dyed red. They make many kinds of baskets and cane vessels lined with raw rubber for carrying water. *Nocte, Wancho* and *Monpa* tribes are expert in wood carving and painting. Tribes of Arunachal Pradesh are expert in their loom and produce colourful textile garments of wide varieties. They used to prepare dyes from different indigenous herbs found in their locality. Woven magnificent carpets of West Kameng and West Siang, woven rugs of the *Adis* area, **Mishmis** bags and shawls, wood carving of Tirap and Kameng are of high commercial demand and value.

Tribes of Arunachal Pradesh are not known to extract metals from metallic ores but there is enough information about the art of alloy making and fine metal works like ornaments, weapon and other objects of art. As per *Nishing* folklore *Nya Loma* (son of *Abotani*) was the pioneer of the art of metallurgical science. These craft men of Adi, Apatani and Nishi tribe ascend to their position by way of hard labour and gaining experience.

**Bibliography**

1. Singh, K.A. (2002). Research Management Perspective of Arunachal Agriculture. ICAR Research Complex for NEH Region, A.P. Centre, Basar

2. Haridasan K, Shukla GP, Benewal BS (1989). Medicinal Plants of Arunachal Pradesh. SFRI Information Bulletin, No.5. State Forest Research Institute, Itanagar

3. Hegde SN (2002). Arunachal Pradesh State Biodiveristy Stretagy & Action Plan – Final Report. State Forest Research Institute, Itanagar

4. SAPCC (2011). Arunachal Pradesh State Action Plan on Climate Change. Department of Environment and Forest. Government of Arunachal Pradesh. Itanagar

**Authors:**

Mr. Kaushik Bhagawati (Research Associate)

Dr. Rupankar Bhagawati (Joint Director)

Dr. Doni Jini (Scientist)

Dr. Rajesh A. Alone (Scientist)

Mr. Raghuver Singh (Scientist)

Dr. Anup Chandra (Scientist)